I0102049

The Continuum of Transformation

Cheryl Miller

Copyright © 2012, 2018 by Cheryl Miller.
Revised 2026. All rights reserved. Printed
in the United States of America. No part of
this book may be used or reproduced in
any manner whatsoever without written
permission except in the case of brief
quotations embodied in critical articles and
reviews.

ISBN 978-0-9859546-2-8

With special thanks
and in honor of
my sweet friend Felecia

Robby Burdge and I were friends for a long time. We met at a fundraising dinner for the small nonprofit housing program I ran for women. That meeting began our long-term partnership to create a program helping women and their children start new lives. With his leadership, our nonprofit grew stronger, and we explored new ways to help women in our program overcome what seemed like insurmountable obstacles.

This collaboration led to the Center for Peace, a women-run social enterprise in our home that offered job training and helped launch small businesses through microloans. We witnessed dramatic transformations, with earnings increasing by up to 157% and several women starting successful businesses.

I remember sitting with Robby at lunch at Victoria Country Club. We marveled at the progress. I said, we should craft language about what we're seeing and why. If we describe the transformation, we can share it with others.

Robby pulled out a napkin. "Okay, let's map this out." We talked and hashed it out. And twenty minutes later, the Continuum of Transformation was revealed. Seeing the diagram—first on that cocktail napkin, now in this book—I saw how truly profound these concepts are.

Robby passed away on May 5, 2025. He dedicated his life to loving and caring for his family, coworkers, friends, and community, leaving lasting legacies that continue to inspire us. One of those legacies was captured on a small cocktail napkin and became the words of this book.

My gratitude for Robby Burdge runs deep. His friendship and wisdom were gifts that changed my life.

This book is dedicated to his faithfulness in loving others and his community.

The Continuum of Transformation

Bianca sat stiffly in her chair amid the clutter of the small office. The muscles in her jaw and chest were clenched tight and she narrowed her eyes to stare at Miss Annette.

She watched Miss Annette's mouth moving and heard some of her words, but when she heard the words "rules" and "authority" that familiar tightness intensified in her chest as if she was being wound like a coil.

Bianca was about to explode when Miss Annette said gently, "You can do this. You are a good mother."

With those words the dam broke. Just a moment before the rage that threatened to explode now came rushing out as tears and sobbing. She was crying like a baby and she really didn't care. She was just so tired. Not just tired, but exhausted.

She and her brothers and sisters had been raised in poverty and drugs. Her mother had been raised in poverty and drugs. It was all she really knew. Bianca believed that being poor was not just her situation but who she was.

In that moment in the office with Miss Annette, Bianca set her mind to change. It was time to stop running. She knew she had to make changes in her life for herself and her sons.

Later that night, she lay in the dark and she prayed to a God she had just met a few days earlier. She prayed awkward words but knew somehow it was right.

She thought about her family growing up. Her mother's family was originally from Mexico. Her parents told stories of traditions and superstitions about life growing up in rural Mexico. Her mother told Bianca the story about how she had been told to get a "Sancho" when she was twelve. Bianca knew exactly what that meant. They were creepy men who called and would request "things;" then when the *Sancho* left the family would have extra money for food or shoes or whatever they needed. How could a mother make her thirteen-year-old daughter take on a *Sancho*? Bianca loved her mother and as much as she wished she could disobey, she knew she had no choice.

A week later her mother announced, "I have found you a *Sancho*. Go to the back room and wait."

When the older man came over she felt the heat in her cheeks go up several degrees as she looked at his repulsive distorted smile. She did what he asked. Afterward, the *Sancho* took his camera, paid her mother, and left.

The memory of her first day with her *Sancho* replayed in Bianca's mind as she lay on her bed that first night at the home. She just couldn't make sense of how she felt. Then, she realized that she had always had the nightmares and fears but she had never had them in a place where she felt safe in spite of them. Yes, this was different. That difference, she decided would be the hope she would cling to. If she could pull this off, her boys would never have to be where she was now lying in a bed with fearful memories clinging to a thread of hope that life could be better. She finally drifted off to sleep clutching that hope...

"I pray u get hit by a truck and dragd for miles. Next time u need a cake on ur birthday call me, but I cant promise it won't be rat poison!"

This was a post on my Facebook page by my friend Bianca. I met her when she moved into the housing program I ran, my place of employment. Bianca's journey took her from being a ninth-grade dropout to a crack house to sobriety then back to a crack house. Unfortunately, this cycle is all too common with women who attempt to leave addiction and poverty.

Bianca once told me, "My mom was born into poverty; I was born into poverty, and that's just the way life was. There was no getting over it; no getting better. That is just the way life was."

Or so she thought before she came to our housing program. In her time at the home she learned that she did have choices and amazing talent. She began the journey out of chaos then she slipped back into negative behaviors that culminated in the outburst and threats posted on Facebook. Within days she was back in the crack house and full-blown addiction. Unfortunately for many, the story would end there. But it didn't for Bianca.

A few weeks later she realized how much she had lost. She also realized that she was simply not the crack addict from generational poverty anymore. There was no undoing the fact that she had experienced success in her sober life. Sitting at a desk, dressed as a professional, answering the phone with a sophisticated voice, Bianca knew she was no longer the girl from the hood. No undoing the discovery that she had found many untapped gifts and strengths. So, on her own, she began to crawl back out of the darkness. A year later, Bianca learned how to drive, got her license, got her GED, and is now a full-time college student.

So how does a person go from a crack house to college? What can we learn from the experiences of women like Bianca?

For the past 15 years, we have worked with women from the most extreme situations of generational poverty, lifetime addictions, and repeated sentences in prison. And thankfully, more often than not, we have seen the results like those experienced by Bianca.

There are actually two processes that occur as people move toward transformation. The first is a linear process of phases that people will experience when trying to rebuild a life that has crumbled. Bianca moved into the home. Her life was in chaos. After a few days, she settled in and began to evaluate her life, as people do in the survival phase. She was provided job skills training to help move her toward stability. All these steps were a linear progression toward a new future.

The second is more of an internal process we go through when trying to change negative behaviors. Bianca moved into our housing program, decided to start over and made positive steps. Yet, as you will see with the rest of her story, moving into the home in and of itself did not bring all Bianca's negative addictive behaviors to stop immediately.

These two processes combined become the continuum of transformation.

This continuum is not limited to people with negative lifestyles. It appears to be more universal, and we all move through this continuum to some degree.

A person experiences a chaotic event like the death of a loved one or loss of income. She (or he) copes by striving to survive, eventually moving from chaos toward some level of survival, then on to stability. Once stable, the opportunity to move into a more dynamic future is achievable. The diagram below illustrates this continuum of transformation.

Chaos　　Survival　　　Stability　　　　　　　Dynamic

└──────┴────────────┴──────────────────────→

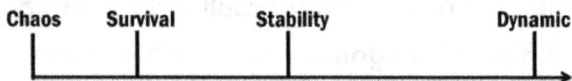

The goal in working with people in any situation where change is expected should be to create an environment, or a road map, that is most conducive to moving people forward in the continuum of transformation. There is a scripture in the Old Testament where Isaiah tells the people to do just that.[1]

"Go out! Go out! Prepare the roadway for my people to return! Build the roads, pull out the boulders, raise the flag of Israel. See, the Lord has sent his messengers to every land and said, 'Tell my people, I, the Lord your God, am coming to save you and will bring you many gifts.' And they shall be called 'The

---

[1] Isaiah 62:10-12 (TLB)

Holy People' and 'The Lord's Redeemed,' and Jerusalem shall be called 'The Land of Desire' and 'The City God Has Blessed.'"

The people of Israel were in exile. Life was chaos, or at best, they were surviving. But God calls them to redemption, to something more. The means to get from one place to another was for a highway to be built, for the way to be prepared. We can create this same type of opportunity today for people seeking more. If we take this scripture and lay it over the continuum of transformation, we begin to see the simple diagram in a different way.

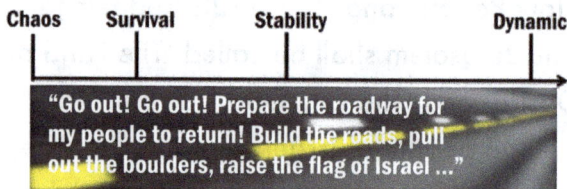

| Chaos | Survival | Stability | Dynamic |

"Go out! Go out! Prepare the roadway for my people to return! Build the roads, pull out the boulders, raise the flag of Israel ..."

As Christians, our task is to "build" this highway for people to return. How do we remove boulders for people? How do we create this highway? The ways can be as varied as people, and we begin by evaluating external barriers people encounter, as well as internal negative behaviors. Facilitating reconciliation for past harms is a major "boulder" that can be removed. Addressing addictive behaviors to prevent future harm is another way to help people return to a healthy life.

It is the responsibility of the individual to choose to move toward transformation. When a person returns to her (or his) true calling, she (or he) begins to function in the ways in which God intended. When she (he) lives in the fullness of the life God created, she (he) operates in the dynamic. So how do we build this highway to create the greatest possible opportunity for success and the living of the life that Jesus references?

"My purpose is to give life in all its fullness." John 10:10 (TLB)

It is important to begin to understand the characteristics of each phase of the continuum of transformation. It is also important to know what elements must be in place for an individual to transition from one phase to the next.

The individual must put some of the elements in place. Other elements are external, implemented by those who journey alongside those seeking transformation.

Chaos

When a person experiences chaos, life is out of control. Nothing makes sense. Everything that once seemed to help maintain some sense of life has ceased to work. Often destructive patterns are magnified in this phase. If patterns or behaviors like binge drinking, attractions to unhealthy relationships, violence, or criminal activity exist they can intensify when life is in chaos. Relationships are strained to the utmost if not absent altogether. There is no sense of order,

right or wrong, just ongoing pandemo-
nium. It is usually in the phase of chaos
that most people will experience their
"rock bottom." To define rock bottom is
literally impossible since it is directly tied
to individual lifestyles. Wherever "rock
bottom" is found, the fact is, once there, a
person will take stock and decide if it is
time to climb out of chaos or not. Most of
the time, it is necessary that the individual
wants a change. To make the shift from
one phase to another an individual has to
choose to move forward. Yet, chaos is the
one phase where it is possible for outside
forces to step in and address the problem.
This is most evident in drug and criminal
behavior. It is common for addicts to
remain in chaos and never find her or his
"rock bottom." If left on their own some
addicts would stay in their destructive

lifestyle until death, and many do. Yet there are times when outside forces stop the chaos, even if momentarily. This happens most commonly when those in addiction are arrested. The outside authority comes in and removes the person from the chaos. Once in a different, more constrained environment the individual may have a moment of clarity and decide to move toward change and rebuilding a life.

Falling into chaos is not limited to addiction. It can be seen in situations where people find themselves in chaos due to circumstances outside their control, like the death of a loved one or loss of employment. When the chaos is caused by outside circumstances, not personal choices, the individual will arrive at that moment where she or he says, "enough is enough" and begin looking for ways to move out of this phase.

For a person to move out of chaos toward the survival phase, three elements are required: structure, rules, and order. Structure is created when elements are logically arranged in a system that is discernible and reflects an intentional purpose. Rules are a common set of regulations providing predictability. Order is different than structure and rules in that the first two simply exist. Order happens when structure and rules are put into action.

One of the women living in our housing program put this concept into words quite succinctly: "My life was spinning out of control and it was as if you grabbed me by my shoulders and said, 'STOP!'"

This woman had made the choice to leave her chaotic lifestyle and moved into our housing program, which is intentional about creating a place that has structure, rules, and order. Providing this type of environment allows the individual to stop and evaluate what changes need to be made and what steps are needed to move forward. The more confining the environment in this early transition, the more likely the individual will have time to evaluate and make decisions.

On her first day sitting on the bunk in a women's dorm, in prison for the fifth time, Sarah knew something needed to change. She knew she had time to think and decided to make different choices when she left.

Although being in a confining lifestyle is necessary to evaluate and make decisions, it can become a hindrance if a person remains in that situation for too long. Structure, rules, and order can be maintained throughout all phases of transformation, yet, that narrow place of intense structure is only needed for a short period of time. Going back to the example of jail or prison, the time in that confined space can provide an individual the opportunity to evaluate and take stock in the lifestyle that led to the confinement. However, it is common knowledge that jail and/or prison for long time periods can actually increase the original behavior problems.

The same is true for less serious situations. For this reason, our housing program operated in a system where individuals have little freedom or privileges when first entering the program.

The first most confining phase is very brief, only a few days. It is intentionally designed to allow people to have that moment of clarity to evaluate and make some basic decisions of what needs to happen to move forward. Restrictions are quickly lessened, and done so incrementally, because individuals need to take responsibility for their lifestyles and learn to create order and structure themselves. Learning to create and build their own rules and structure will allow them to move out of chaos and to the next phase of survival. If the responsibility is not shifted to the individual, that person will always be dependent on others to ensure their life is in control. The goal should always be to move people to independence and the fullness of who God has created each of them to be.

Survival

The survival phase is characterized by "barely enough." There is barely enough in place to maintain order and structure. The distance between chaos and survival is very short and it is best if individuals move from one to the other quickly. Staying in survival phase puts an individual at risk of falling back into chaos at any given moment. When an individual experiences survival stage directly after leaving chaos, it brings hope. When there are even a few resources in place to maintain order, an individual experiences hope that the process of transformation can occur. Those resources can be both internal and external. Internal resources include determination, willingness, maintaining sobriety, etc. External resources could be assistance from others, a job, a temporary place to live, etc.

For a person to go beyond survival and move toward stability, the elements required are limited appropriate assistance, external consistency, and time. Appropriate limited resources would be outside resources that the individual would not have access to otherwise. Resources can take on many forms. It can be training to increase earning potential. It can be an opportunity to continue education.

Without some form of appropriate limited assistance from an outside source, individuals may be forced to stay in survival mode.

External consistency is also required, with help by whatever individual, program, or entity that is providing the structure and order from the chaos phase.

The consistency creates a pattern for the individual to learn and eventually adapt in the next phase. And of course, time is required so habits and healthy changes have the ability to develop.

And time in needed to begin developing new behaviors.

Angela arrived by bus from prison with all her belongings in a white sack and a check from parole for $50 to start her new life. When Angela arrived, she was determined to do things different. Over the next six months she demonstrated consistency of new healthy behaviors. All the determination in the world, though, would not get her from the bus station that rainy December morning and provide her home for the next six months for only $50. Her new start required limited assistance in the form of a ride to her new home, a place to live as she got back on her feet, and food and support as she began her journey.

A single mom making minimum wage can work for years and maintain sobriety for years but without appropriate limited assistance, she may never leave survival mode. Angela was a single mom. She did maintain her sobriety and she was diligent in working consistently. But her lack of a high school diploma and felony conviction meant her only job choices were minimum wage. Angela did save enough to get her own place, but the $500 car she purchased earlier that year broke down and her savings was depleted. Not long after, she lost a week of work due to the flu and had no reserve this time and lost her apartment. She returned to our program. This time she went back to school to get her GED. The limited outside resources of literacy and temporary housing allowed Angela to find a higher paying job and maintain economic stability upon leaving the program.

The longer a person stays in the survival stage, the greater the risk that outside circumstances will cause a plummet back into chaos.

The need to recognize appropriate limited assistance is critical. The assistance must bridge the gap between dependency and autonomy. The way to determine this is simple. If the assistance provided forces the individual to depend on that resource to maintain their lifestyle indefinitely, it is not appropriate. (Welfare is the best example of dependency.) Providing an outside resource without a plan to move toward autonomy only creates a trap and can shatter a person's resolve to try to make changes.

So, outside resources are required but the other elements of external consistency, and time must also be in place. If there is no willingness for a person to maintain consistency, those providing the external support are wasting valuable resources.

Stability

The next phase is stability. Stability is characterized by implementing healthy routines of successful daily living. It is the process of getting up each day, going to work or school, coming home, interacting with family, going to sleep and starting all over again the next day. While each day may hold new experiences, the idea is that there is a routine and pattern that is fairly common. This is a phase where, for

most people, that
the majority of life is lived. There is not
necessarily a need or requirement to move
past stability. In fact, for some people to
achieve and maintain stability is a
significant accomplishment. This stability
phase is characterized by intentional
consistency, time, and mastery that must
be maintained.

The external consistency in the
previous phase becomes internalized in
this phase. Consistency is steadfast
adherence to principles or course of
action. In this context, it is the commitment
to the order that is implemented in the
survival stage. Mastery is when an
individual becomes efficient and adept in
the performance of the activities
implemented in the survival phase. To
become consistent and adept in healthy

patterns, time is required. Doing something once does not constitute mastery of a task. Repeating a behavior over time consistently does. The person must maintain all the resources discovered in survival to ensure moving toward stability. A job is maintained by consistently showing up to work every day, ensuring economic stability. Maintaining sobriety for an addict is done through time and consistency. If these elements are not in place, the person is at risk of falling back into survival, then chaos.

Many people in society live in stability permanently. Individuals who stay in this phase forever have a sense that the day-to-day details of life are the ends to the means. It is not necessarily a bad thing for individuals to maintain this phase their entire lives.

Karen goes to work every day at Dollar General and her husband Tom works construction. They rent a modest home and raise three children.

Juanita works as a nurse in the local hospital. She owns a two-bedroom home. She goes to work every day and takes her daughter to school every day.

Karen, Tom and Juanita are good citizens, providing for their families. They just never ask, "Is there more?" It is not a bad thing they are content; it is just the life they chose. And the truth is, for some people even attaining this phase is miraculous.

Another former resident of named Sarah is a perfect example of the miracle of even moving into this phase of stability. Sarah spent 19 years addicted to heroin and crack. Her chaotic lifestyle led to homelessness and eight felony convictions. Each time she was incarcerated, she had the opportunity to evaluate and decide to make changes, but the dangerous patterns of her past pulled her back to chaos. The fifth time Sarah went to prison, she decided to do things differently. Upon release, she chose to go to our housing program.

After two years, Sarah was maintaining her sobriety, keeping a part-time job, and attending college. After 19 years of serious addiction, to be maintaining a healthy lifestyle of work, school, and sobriety is a miracle!

Most social services focus on the task of moving people from survival to stability. This is an important phase, ensuring the changes that occur can be maintained and allowing for a healthy lifestyle. While this phase is critical, those we work with need to be made aware there is still an option for further growth, further opportunity, and further transformation.

Stability provides a perfect launching point for people to move toward the dynamic phase. Unfortunately, many people misinterpret stability as the completion of transformation.

"But it is just as the Scriptures say,
'What God has planned
    for people who love him
is more than eyes have seen
    or ears have heard.
It has never even
    entered our minds!'"
    1 Cor. 2:9 (CEV)

We can imagine going to work every day and tackling all the world has to offer. We can imagine our children growing up and being healthy and happy. These are the things we can imagine about our lives and

future. Yet, the scripture in Corinthians clearly indicates there is more, that God has greater plans that we cannot even imagine. This is dynamic.

Remember the scripture in John.[2] Jesus came so we could experience "life in all its fullness."

---

[2] John 10:10 (TLB)

Dynamic

Living from the dynamic phase means living from the place where our talents and gifts overlay the vocation or work God has called us to do. It can be characterized as "living the dream." This is not to say that everything in dynamic is rosy. Lots of days,
it is hard! Dynamic can occur when we move into a work environment, or place of service, or ministry that allows us to use all our life experiences, gifts, untapped potential to the fullest. Early on, we may not be able to fully imagine what dynamic looks like, since it is God who created us that knows our visible and hidden gifts.

Moving toward dynamic living requires empowerment, growth, and most importantly, courage.

Bianca's story beautifully demonstrates empowerment. She made the statement, "My mom was born into poverty; I was born into poverty, and that's just the way life was."

This sense of fatalism limited her ability to realize there may be other choices and sitting in an office answering phones she realized she had the power to choose another path. Growth in Bianca's case was demonstrated by the gradual increase in skills working in an office and the development of new behaviors that enabled her to move ahead financially. Yet moving forward meant leaving behind all she had ever known. The fear that arises in making this type of life change shows up in many ways. So many ask, "What if I fail?" "What if I can't do it?"

And many have family members that resist them changing for fear of losing connection. To continue to move toward the unknown facing these fears takes incredible courage. Anytime we transition from one familiar lifestyle to a different unknown lifestyle some level of fear may arise. Courage is the ability to face difficulties and move forward in spite of fear.

Any person working with people in transformation will come to the realization,
"I can't change anyone!" However, we can be intentional about "removing boulders" and "building a highway" so each person recognizes that she (he) is empowered and can choose to continue becoming who God plans for her (him) to be.

The cycles of mastery that are required to maintain stability can become a trap of security. Stability can create predictability. There is a sense of knowing what needs to be done and then getting it done. This becomes comfortable and makes the idea of going for more in life somewhat dangerous. There does need to be a counting of the cost. Moving away from the security of stability is inherently dangerous, particularly for individuals who experienced numerous failures ending in chaos. This is why many people are afraid to dream or dare to take risks. It is not a judgment against someone who does not want to take the risk. There will always be more of life to seek and pursue, and doing so will always mean leaving behind some things that are familiar.

If Sarah had decided to simply maintain a lifestyle of work and sobriety after a life of 20 years in heroin addiction and five trips to prison, we might consider that a miracle. Fortunately, Sarah wanted more. She continued to take risks and push herself. Recently, Sarah married her sweetheart at a fairytale church wedding, and she graduated with a bachelor's degree the following semester. She has also worked to make the community a better place by creating programs that address crime. She has done so much that she has been asked to speak at national conferences to thousands about never giving up on people and never giving up on changing. Sarah is just one story of many of women who are choosing to take risks and to move toward the dynamic life God has planned. When a person lives

dynamically, she (he) embraces the fullness of what God has created her (him) to be
and do.

The continuum of transformation is a linear process that defines how a person moves from Point A (chaos) to Point B (dynamic). A second behavioral spiral process that addresses an individual's personal response to negative and positive behaviors also exists and happens simultaneously.

There is a need to address the behavioral spiral while an individual is moving through the linear process of the continuum of transformation. This behavioral spiral is observed as we walk alongside women in our program. It is not necessarily good or bad, just more of the reality we see demonstrated time and time again.

It is very rare that a woman comes into the home, decides to leave her old lifestyle behind, and completely changes all the behaviors that led her into chaos. In the past 18 years, we have never seen that occur. There may be areas of life that are radically changed and never returned to, like addiction, but there tend to be other negative behaviors accompanying the lifestyle that need to be addressed. The process of changing behavior tends to be cyclical.

The negative behavioral spiral   is what causes individuals to end up in chaos to begin with. The common description of this process is that life rapidly spirals out of control until someone hits "rock bottom."

It is important to think about the process that leads to chaos because this behavioral spiral is always happening, whether for the good or for the bad. When circumstances and choices are predominately negative individuals cycle in and out of negative behaviors, making it look like the diagram on the right.

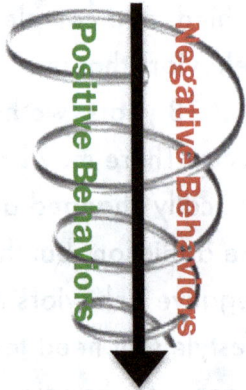

As a society, we seem to have an expectation that when a person hits "rock bottom" she (he) will realize the need for change and simply stop the negative behaviors that led to "rock bottom."

There is almost   an expectation that
the realization of a negative behavior is
the catalyst necessary to stop it. Negative
behaviors lead people's lives to spiral out
of control until they hit "rock bottom."
When a person hits that "rock bottom" the
expectation is that the person will simply
stop the negative behaviors and life will
be restored back to the "top" or place she
(he) was before things started spiraling
downward.

This is not a process limited to
changing negative behaviors that are
dramatic like addiction. How many times
have you committed to eating healthier?
Did you do it for a while then fall back
into unhealthy eating patterns?

There are those rare individuals who
make a change and never go back. But it
is far more common that we implement

new healthier behaviors then have lapses where we cycle back to the unhealthy behaviors. Either way, when the person hits her (his) "rock bottom," whether it is jail or homelessness or the stepping on the scale, she (he) is realizing something needs to be done and the process of change begins. This process of change is not linear like the continuum of transformation. What actually occurs is the exact opposite of the spiral downward to "rock bottom." Individuals will still cycle in and out of constructive and destructive behaviors and decisions.

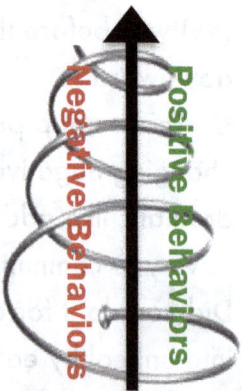

Negative Behaviors

Positive Behaviors

The most critical component in working with people as they rebuild their lives is that there must be forward progress as the cycles occur. As individuals cycle in and out of behaviors, there must be a marked attempt to move out of chaos.

When you overlay these two concepts it really looks more like the following:

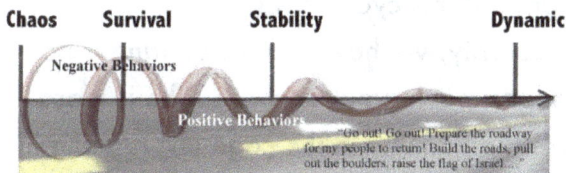

There should be a diminishing of the severity and frequency of the cycles that is more accurately illustrated in the above diagram. It becomes critical to watch as individuals cycle in and out of behaviors to determine if there is a clear attempt to move back toward life before things began to spiral out of control.

For example, Jane's crack addiction leads her to homelessness, her "rock bottom." She gets sober and begins to rebuild her life. The first major obstacle she encounters causes her to relapse. She hits "rock bottom" again and gets sober again. If this cycle repeats itself with regularity, we have to realize Jane is no longer moving out of chaos. She is more like the hamster in the cage just running in circles.

Evidence of progress would be indicated by greater periods of time between relapse, (or less frequency of relapse episodes). If we give up on people when they fall back into negative behaviors, we agree with their unspoken choice that "they can never change." When working with someone addressing destructive behaviors we must learn to distinguish between enabling a person to repeat destructive choices while never really attempting to change, and continuing to work with someone who is trying to move forward even though she (he) stumbles from time to time.

So, there are two ongoing processes happening simultaneously as demonstrated in this final diagram. As we journey to arrive at that place where "no eye has seen and no ear has heard,"[3] we cycle in and out of behaviors and decisions and we progress on the continuum of transformation. Learning to walk alongside others can be a daunting task. What it calls for is to be willing to

---

3 1 Cor 2:9 (CEV)

pull out boulders and build a road within the turbulent winds of a cyclone. No problem, right? This may not be an easy ride but the reward is dynamic!

Phase Overview

The first phase is chaos that requires:

Rules

Structure

Order

The second phase is survival that requires:

Limited Appropriate Assistance

Time

External Consistency

The third phase is stability that requires:

Time

Internal Consistency

Mastery

The final phase is dynamic that requires:

Empowerment

Growth

Courage

Seeing these different phases of transformation and what is required at each stage can be an invaluable tool as we seek change. Because transformation is a part of our everyday life, we are all being transformed daily by circumstances, choices, and life in general. What becomes important is that when we seek to intentionally bring about transformation, we need to understand how it works and what it looks like.

Hopefully, the concepts in this book will become a road map, a guide, and a place to circle back to check where we are on the road to transformation, where we want to be, and how far we have to go.

About the Author

Cheryl Miller owns Cheryl Miller Consulting, LLC, providing transformative training in several areas: nonprofit leadership, economic development, conflict management, and restorative justice. She previously served for eighteen years as the Executive Director of a successful and innovative nonprofit housing program.

Cheryl is the author of *Business Doing Good, Engaging Women and Elevating Communities* (Rowman & Littlefield 2021) and *Enough Silence, Creating Sacred Space for Survivors of Sexual Violence through Restorative Justice* (Eerdman's Publishing 2024)

Her overcomer story was featured in People.com and Adam Carolla's Take a Knee Podcast. Cheryl is also a TEDx TAMU speaker. Cheryl lives in Victoria, Texas, with her husband and chickens and travels as often as possible to see her grown children and grandchildren.

www.cheryldmiller.com